This book belongs to:

_____

I am VERY important to God!

My
BIBLE FRIENDS
Read-and-Do Book

by

Robin Currie

illustrated by

Cecilia Washington Carr

Pauline
BOOKS & MEDIA
BOSTON

Nihil Obstat:
Rev. Thomas W. Buckley, S.T.D., S.S.L.

Imprimatur:
† Bernard Cardinal Law
March 7, 1997

Library of Congress Cataloging-in-Publication Data

Currie, Robin, 1948-
   My Bible friends read-and-do book / by Robin Currie ; illustrated by Cecilia Washington Carr.
      p. cm.
   Summary: An easy-to-read collection of stories about twenty-eight major Old and New Testament figures that contains special messages, prayers, and text-oriented activities.
   ISBN 0-8198-4795-X (cloth).
   1. Bible stories, English. [1. Bible stories.] I. Carr, Cecilia Washington, ill.   II. Title.
BS551.2.C87   1997
220.9'505—dc21   97-14056
                                                                CIP
                                                                AC

Printed and published in the U.S.A. by Pauline Books & Media, 50 St. Paul's Avenue, Boston, MA 02130.

http://www.pauline.org
E-mail: PBM_EDIT@INTERRAMP.COM

Pauline Books & Media is the publishing house of the Daughters of St. Paul, an international congregation of women religious serving the Church with the communications media.

1 2 3 4 5 6 7 8   04 03 02 01 00 99 98 97

To my parents,
Robert and Dorothy Hunt,
who first shared
these stories with me.

Contents

Adam and Eve and the Beginning of the World

At the beginning of the world, there was only God.

Everything else was dark.
(Close your eyes.
That is how dark it was.)

There were no ponies or apples or lakes.

There were no people to ride ponies or eat apples or wade in lakes.

At the beginning of the world, there was only God.

And God began to make everything.

First God made day.

God made the light and the sun.
(Touch your fingertips overhead to make the sun.)

Then God made night.

Next God made the moon and all the stars.
(Can you reach high enough to touch a star?)

God saw that it was very good.
(Look around. It is very good.)

God made the water and dry land.

God put the water in lakes and rivers and the ocean.
God made a few puddles of water, too.
(Do you like to splash in puddles?)

God made some dry, flat land for growing food.

God made some land into mountains with snow at the top.
*(Touch your fingertips together in front of your nose.
Are you bigger than the mountain?)*

God saw that it was very good.
(Look around. It is very good.)

First there was God.

Then God made ponies and apples and lakes.

But there was still no one to ride the ponies or eat the apples or wade in the lakes.

So God made people like you and me.
(Point to yourself.)

The first people were Adam and Eve.

God told Adam and Eve to take care of everything
he had made.

God told them to take care of the green grass and
yellow chicks.

God told them to take care of the dogs who bark...
(Bark.)

and the bees that buzz.
(Bzzzz.)

God even told them to take care of big gray elephants...
(Wave your arms like an elephant trunk.)

and little gray mice.
(Wiggle your nose like a mouse.)

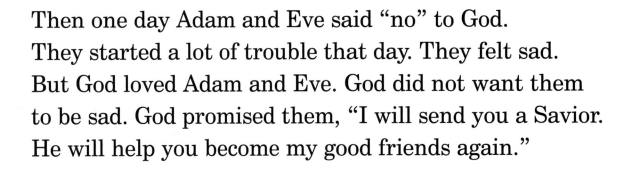

Then one day Adam and Eve said "no" to God.
They started a lot of trouble that day. They felt sad.
But God loved Adam and Eve. God did not want them
to be sad. God promised them, "I will send you a Savior.
He will help you become my good friends again."

Adam and Eve say...

God made everything, big and little, loud and quiet, near and far. God made people to care for everything. How do you help take care of God's world?

Say a prayer with Adam and Eve

Dear God, I love your wonderful world.
Help me take good care of it. Amen.

Fun with Adam and Eve

Get a big piece of paper and your crayons.
Can you draw all the things mentioned in the story?
What other things do you like to draw?

Noah's Big Ark

Once when God looked at the world, God was sad.

(Make a sad, sad face.)

People were forgetting to be kind. They were doing many wrong things.

And so God decided to give the world a new beginning. God made it rain and rain.

(Wiggle your fingers overhead for the rain.)

Earth would be covered with water. There would be no people, no dogs or elephants, no yellow chicks.

(Shake your head no.)

But God chose to save a man named Noah and his family. God did not want Noah and his family to be under the water.

So God told Noah to build a big ark. An ark is a great big boat.

(Hold your arms out to show "big.")

Noah sawed the wood.

(Pretend to saw some wood.)

He hammered the boards together.
(Pound with a hammer.)

Whew! It was hard work!
At last the animals came onto the ark, two at a time.
(Count the animals: 1-2.)

There were two lions.
(Roar like a lion.)

There were big animals like the elephant.
(What does an elephant's trunk look like?)

There were small animals like the cat.
(Say "meow." Can you purr, too?)

There were teeny-weeny animals like the caterpillar
(Wiggle your fingers up your arm. That tickles!)

and animals like the kangaroo who hopped.
(Hop.)

It started to rain.
(Wiggle two fingers overhead for a little rain.)

It rained and rained and rained. What a storm!
(Wiggle all your fingers.)

The wind blew.
(Blow and blow and blow.)

The thunder was loud.
(Quick! Cover your ears!)

But God kept the people and animals safe in the ark.

At last the sun began to shine.
(Touch your fingertips overhead to make the sun.)

The flood was over. Hooray!

Bump!
(Clap your hands.)

The ark stopped on the top of a mountain.

Noah opened the doors of the ark.

The tall giraffes came out.
(Point to your long neck.)

Then came the wiggly worms.
(Can you wiggle like a worm?)

Last came the slow animals like the turtles.
(Wave "good-bye" to the slow turtles.)

18

Then Noah's family saw a rainbow up in the sky.
(What colors do you know?)

The rainbow was God's promise:
there would never be another flood.

Noah and his family said "thank you" to God.
(Fold your hands to say "thank you" to God.)

Noah says...

God takes care of you, too, by giving you a home and family. Sometimes a storm may be loud and scary, but God will keep you safe, just like God kept me, my family and all the animals safe in the ark.

Say a prayer with Noah

Dear God, thank you for taking good care of Noah and his family and all the animals. Thank you for taking good care of me! Amen.

Fun with Noah

Cut pictures from magazines or draw different animals. Paste them on the inside of a shoe box for your own Noah's ark.

Sarah Laughs

Once a man named Abraham lived in a place called Haran with his wife Sarah.

Then God told Abraham and Sarah to move from their home to a new place.

They put all their things in boxes for the long trip.

They took all the cows.
(Moooo.)

They took all the sheep.
(What do sheep say?)

All of Abraham and Sarah's relatives went to the new place too.

They went where God told Abraham to go.

They had to walk a long way.
(Tap your hands on your knees a long time.)

Then they walked even more.
(Tap hands on knees a long, long time.)

The cows and sheep were tired.
(Moooo. Baaaa.)

Abraham and Sarah and all the people were tired.
(Rest your head on your hands.)

God showed Abraham and Sarah
a new and beautiful place to live.
(Shade your eyes to see far away to the new place.)

There was good grass for the cows.
(Moooo.)

There was a place for everyone to build houses.
(Pretend to hammer.)

Abraham and Sarah were very happy in the new place.
(Smile your happiest smile.)

Later on when Sarah was an old, old woman
and Abraham was an old, old man, God blessed them
in a special way. God promised to send them a baby.
(Fold your arms to rock a baby.)

When Sarah heard God's promise, she laughed.
She thought she was much too old to have a baby.

Sarah had to learn that God can do everything!

God kept his promise. Very soon Sarah had a baby.
(Fold your arms to rock a baby.)

Abraham and Sarah loved their baby Isaac very much.

Later God promised that one day Abraham would have
more children than the stars in the sky!
(Point to the sky.)

When Isaac grew up he had children
and those children had children.
(Hold up one finger, then two, then five, then ten!)

But the Bible also tells us that everyone who believes in
God as Abraham did is part of Abraham's family.
So Abraham's family had as many children
as there were stars in the sky.
(That's too many to count!)

God kept his promises to Abraham and Sarah.

God always keeps his promises. You can count on that!

Sarah and Abraham say...

God loves you very much. God wants you to trust him. God keeps his promises and does wonderful things for everyone who trusts him!

Say a prayer with Sarah and Abraham

Dear God, thank you for my home and family. Help me to love and trust you more and more. Amen.

Fun with Sarah and Abraham

Look around your room. If you were going on a trip like Sarah and Abraham in the story, what would you take? Would it all fit in one box?

Jacob Comes Home

When Isaac grew up he married Rebekah. They lived in a place called Canaan and had twin boys named Jacob and Esau.

(Hold up two fingers.)

The twins didn't look alike or like the same things.

Esau was his father's favorite. Jacob was his mother's favorite.

One day, with his mother's help, Jacob took something that belonged to Esau. Esau got very angry.
He wanted to punish Jacob.

(Make an angry face.)

So Rebekah sent Jacob far away to keep him safe.

Jacob did not come back for a long, long time.

Jacob was so tired that night
that he slept with a rock for a pillow.

Then he dreamed about a long ladder that reached all the way to the sky.

(Reach as high as you can.)

Jacob dreamed that the ladder went up to heaven.
There were angels on it.
Up and down they went, serving God.
(Raise and lower your hand—up and down.)

God said, "You must serve me, too, Jacob. And I will be
with you always. Do not be afraid of anything."
Jacob felt much better after that dream.
(Smile.)

Later on, Jacob had a family of his own.

He had cattle and sheep and goats.
He had lots of people around him.
(Point to some of the people around you.)

Then God told him to go back to Canaan.

So Jacob packed up all his things.
His family packed their things.

His cattle and sheep and goats were ready to go.

Jacob set out for home.

But one night Jacob got worried. If he went back
to Canaan he would meet his brother Esau.

Suppose Esau was still angry
and didn't want to see Jacob and his family?

What should Jacob do?
(Shrug your shoulders.)

God sent an angel to remind Jacob
that God would be with him.

Jacob did not need to be afraid.

Finally it was time to meet Esau.

Jacob knew that God was with him.
So Jacob was not afraid.
(Smile.)

Jacob saw Esau coming. Closer and closer he came.
Jacob looked at his face.

Esau was smiling! Esau had missed Jacob!
(Do you think the brothers hugged each other?)

The brothers were glad to be together again.
God was always with them, just like God
is always with you.

Jacob says...

Sometimes friends or even brothers and sisters fight.
Then they feel sad. God never wants you to fight.
God always wants you to love! God understands
that it's hard to love others sometimes.
But remember, God can help you do it!

Say a prayer with Jacob

*Dear God, I want to be kind and loving to everyone.
Please help me to say I'm sorry whenever I do things
that hurt other people. Please help me to forgive people
who hurt me. Amen.*

Fun with Jacob

Pretend you are Jacob. What will
you do when you see Esau
again? What will you say
to Esau?

Joseph and His Brothers

Jacob had 12 sons.
(Count 1-2-3-4-5-6-7-8-9-10-11-12.)

Sometimes he did nice things for one son. The other sons did not like that.
(Make an angry face.)

One time Jacob gave a special coat to his son Joseph. It had many beautiful colors.
(What colors can you name?)

When Joseph showed the coat to his brothers, they were not happy. They wanted to get rid of Joseph.
(Point out the door.)

Then Joseph told them about his dream. In the dream Joseph was the king and his brothers bowed to him.
(Bow.)

That made the other brothers angry. Now they really wanted to get rid of Joseph.
(Point out the door.)

So the brothers made a plan.
They took the colored coat away from Joseph.

They sold Joseph to some men who were going far, far
away. The men were going on camels all the way to Egypt.
(Do you know what a camel has on its back?)

The men took Joseph with them.
(Wave good-bye to Joseph.)

Then the brothers tricked their father Jacob. They made
him think that Joseph was dead. Jacob was very, very sad.
(Make a very sad face.)

 Joseph had many adventures in Egypt.
He became a good friend and helper of the
king. Then Joseph had another dream.
(Rest your head on your hands.)

He dreamed there would be a lot of food grown
for seven years.
(Rub your tummy—lots to eat.)

Then for seven years there would be no food at all.
(Shake your head no.)

Joseph had the people save food during the seven
good years. So when the seven bad years came,
there was plenty to eat.
(Rub your tummy.)

But Jacob and his sons were hungry and Jacob sent his
sons to Egypt to ask for food.

In Egypt, they bowed low to the king's helper.
They did not know they were bowing
to their brother Joseph.
(Bow.)

When they found out that the king's helper was Joseph,
and that he was an important man, they were afraid.

But Joseph said, "I forgive you. God took a bad thing that
happened to me and made it good for all of us.
I have enough food for everyone."

Then Jacob and all of his sons lived
together and the brothers were
friends again.

Joseph says...

God can turn bad things into good things.
God has a special plan just for you.
God always knows and does what is best for you.

Say a prayer with Joseph

Dear God, thank you for my loving family.
Help us to always forgive each other
when we make mistakes. Amen.

Fun with Joseph

Use your crayons to cover a paper with colored stripes like the stripes on Joseph's coat. Fold another paper in half. Cut half a circle on the fold. Open the paper with the cut-out circle and place it over the colored paper to see a beautiful ball. Move the top paper to see the ball change colors.

Moses Has Many Adventures

When Moses was a baby, there was a mean king in Egypt. The king was not happy that so many of the Jewish people were living in Egypt. The king decided to kill all the Jewish baby boys.

(Booooo! Hiss!)

So Moses' mother had to hide him. She put him in a big basket. Then she floated the basket down the river.

(Sing "Row, Row, Row Your Boat" for baby Moses.)

The king's daughter found the basket. She kept Moses for her own son so the king would not hurt him.

(Rock baby Moses. He is safe now.)

When Moses grew up he left the king's house. He went to the desert. There he saw a bush that was on fire but never burned up.

God spoke to Moses from the bush. God wanted Moses to help the Jewish people run away from the mean king.

At first, Moses said, "No, it's too hard."

(Shake your head no.)

God said, "I will always be with you."

Then Moses said, "Yes, I will go back to Egypt
and help the Jewish people get away."
(Nod yes.)

God helped Moses and the people escape,
but the army of Egypt chased after them.

The people ran until they came to the Red Sea.
There was no bridge, and the water was too wide
to swim across.
(Can you swim a long way?)

Moses climbed on a rock and held out
the big stick he carried.
(Hold out your arms.)

Suddenly there was a dry path in the middle of the water!
(Put your hands together in front of you. Pull them apart.)

Now it was safe for the people to cross to the other side.
When the army of Egypt came, the water rushed back.
(Put your hands back together again.)

The army couldn't get across the water.
Moses and the people were safe.

 The people traveled in the desert for a long time.
(Tap your hands on your knees.)

There was no food or water. They were hungry and thirsty.
(Rub your stomach.)

God told Moses to hit a rock with his big stick.
(Clap.)

Water came right out of the rock! Every day God covered the ground with a special bread called manna.
It was good food for the hungry people.

Then Moses climbed Mount Sinai to talk to God.
God gave Moses ten very special rules to help the people love God and one another. These very special rules are called the Ten Commandments.
(Hold up ten fingers.)

When we keep the Ten Commandments we are happy.
God is happy too!

Moses says...

Even if your adventures don't include burning bushes and the army of Egypt, God will always be with you.

Say a prayer with Moses

*Dear God, thank you for giving us your
Ten Commandments. These special rules
teach me how to love you and other people.
Help me to always obey them with love. Amen.*

Fun with Moses

Make a baby Moses out of clay or cut a baby shape out of paper. Put him in a plastic butter tub or bowl and float him in a sink or bathtub.

Joshua and the Promised Land

When Moses helped God's people escape from Egypt, he took them to the desert. They walked there for a long, long time.

(Tap your hands on your knees a long time.)

Finally they came to the Jordan River.

On the other side of the river was the land God had promised they could have. They were almost home!

(Shade eyes to see far away.)

The desert was dry and rocky with lots of sand.

The Promised Land had trees and plenty of water.

The people were glad they had come to the end of the trip.

Moses did not cross the Jordan River with the others. He named a new leader for the people. The leader was Joshua.

Joshua was young and brave.
He looked across the Jordan River
and wanted the land to be his home.

Then he saw a big city with high walls all around.
(How high can you reach?)

The big city was called Jericho.

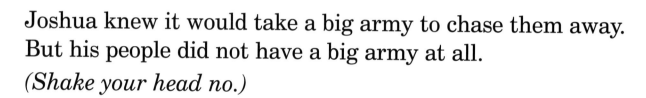

There were people living in Jericho.
They did not want to leave.

Joshua knew it would take a big army to chase them away.
But his people did not have a big army at all.
(Shake your head no.)

So God showed Joshua another way.

Early in the morning the people crossed the Jordan River.
They stood outside the walls of Jericho.
When Joshua gave the signal,
everyone clapped and cheered.
(Clap and cheer loudly.)

Some people blew trumpets as loud as they could.
(Ta-ta-ta!)

They marched around the city of Jericho seven times making all that noise.
(Hold up seven fingers.)

They sounded like a huge army!

Joshua and his noisy little army did this for six days.
On the morning of the seventh day, they came up to the city gates. All of a sudden, they blew the trumpets.
(Blaaaat!)

Then they looked at the big walls.
(Hold your hands up high.)

They heard the sound of cracking. The walls fell down.
(Let your hands drop to the ground.)

The big walls were nothing but a pile of dust.
(Blow away the dust—poof.)

The people inside ran away. The long trip for Joshua and the people was over. At last they were at home in the Promised Land.
(Hooray!)

Joshua says...

Sometimes a job can seem too big for someone small like you. Ask God to help you find the best way to do whatever you have to do.

Say a prayer with Joshua

Dear God, thank you for all the good ideas you give us! I want to always use my ideas to serve you and to help others. Amen.

Fun with Joshua

Build a big wall in a safe place using toy blocks or empty boxes. Blow through a paper towel tube as you march around the wall like Joshua and the people did in the story. Then knock the wall down.

Hannah Makes a Promise

Hannah had a nice house and a good husband. She liked to cook and grow a garden. But Hannah was sad.
(Make a sad face.)

More than anything she wanted a little baby of her own.

Hannah went to the temple of the Lord at Shiloh to pray.
(Fold your hands to pray.)

A man named Eli was there, serving God. He watched Hannah pray.

Eli told Hannah that God heard her prayers and would answer them.

Hannah promised that if God gave her a son, she would let him grow up serving God all his life.

Hannah went home and waited.

Soon God sent Hannah a baby boy.
(Rock the baby.)

She named him Samuel.

Samuel liked to help in the garden and play
with his pet goat.
(Do you have a pet?)

One day Samuel was old enough to serve God.

Hannah got up early and helped Samuel
put on his clothes.

Hannah had made him a brand new coat.
(Can you zip your coat? Zippppp!)

Hannah and Samuel had to walk
a long way to the temple at Shiloh.
(Tap your hands on your knees a long time.)

At the temple Hannah found Eli who served God.

Hannah said to Eli, "God promised me a son,
and God kept that promise.
(Nod yes.)

I promised that my son would serve God,
and now I am keeping my promise.
(Point to yourself like Hannah did.)

Here is my son, Samuel. He will help you serve God."

Soon it was time for Hannah to go home.
She would miss Samuel, but Eli would teach him
and take good care of him.

Hannah kissed Samuel good-bye and went home.
(Tap your hands on your knees.)

Hannah loved Samuel, and she missed him. She did not
forget Samuel because he was away from home.
(Shake your head no.)

Hannah had a plan.

Every year she visited Samuel at the temple.
Every year he grew taller and taller.
(Reach up high.)

The coat she had made him was too small.
(Do you have any clothes that are too small?)

So every year Hannah brought him a new coat.
She made the coats because she loved Samuel.
(Hug yourself.)

Hannah says...

God will answer your prayers in the way that's best for you. Whenever you make a promise to God or anyone else, be sure to keep it.

Say a prayer with Hannah

Dear God, thank you for my mother.
Thank you for her love and for all the
special things she does for me. Amen.

Fun with Hannah

Do you have any old baby clothes around? Try putting on a baby sock. Is it too small for you? If it is, you're just like Samuel, who outgrew his coat. Do you know a baby who could wear the clothes that don't fit you any longer?

A Job for Samuel

Samuel lived at the temple. Sometimes he helped with the cleaning. Sometimes he carried things for Eli. Eli was his teacher and friend.

One night Eli and Samuel were asleep.
(Rest your head on your hands.)

In the middle of the night, Samuel heard Eli call him.
(Touch your ear to listen like Samuel did.)

At least he thought it was Eli calling.
But when Samuel went to Eli, the teacher said,
"Go back to bed. I did not call you."
(Shake your head no.)

So Samuel went back to bed.
(Rest your head on your hands.)

A little later, Samuel heard a voice call him again.
(Touch your ear.)

He went to Eli. But Eli said, "Go back to bed.
I did not call you."
(Shake your head no.)

Then Samuel heard someone call him a third time.
(Touch your ear.)

This time Eli said, "I think God is calling you, Samuel. Next time, say, 'Here I am, Lord.'"

 When Samuel heard his name called again, he said, "Here I am, Lord."
(Say it with Samuel, "Here I am, Lord.")

Then God told Samuel to work in the temple.
God also wanted Samuel to help choose a new king.

When Samuel grew up God spoke to him again.
God told him to go choose the next king.

But Samuel did not know how to choose a king.
(Shake your head no.)

God promised to go with Samuel and help him.

Samuel went to Jesse's farm. Jesse had many sons.
One of them would be the king.

Samuel met the first son.
(Hold up one finger.)

He was strong.
(Make a fist.)

 But God did not choose him to be king.
(Shake your head no.)

Samuel met the second son.
(Hold up two fingers.)

He was smart.
(Point to your head.)

 But God did not choose him to be king.
(Shake your head no.)

Samuel looked at all the sons, but God did not choose
any of them. Jesse said, "My last son, David,
is taking care of the sheep."

When Samuel saw David, God said, "This is the
one who will be king."

Samuel said, "David, you will be the new king.
Take care of the sheep for now. God will take care of you
until it is time to be king."

Samuel says...

When we pray, we let God show us what he wants us to do. We talk to God when we pray. We also listen as God talks to us in our heart.

Say a prayer with Samuel

Dear God, please show me the best way to serve you. Amen.

Fun with Samuel

Fold a paper in half the long way. On one side draw jewels and colored squares. Bring the ends of the paper together with the colors on the outside. Staple or tape them together. This can be your crown for David. Pretend to be Samuel and crown someone king just for fun.

David Is Brave

When David was a boy, he took care of the sheep.
(Baaaa.)

Most days he sang and played his harp. Everything was very quiet.
(Shhhh.)

One day a lion sneaked up behind a big rock. Quietly it got ready to pounce.

David saw the lion's tail behind the rock.
He grabbed a big stick and ran toward the lion.
(Tap your hands on your knees fast for running.)

The lion could have eaten David in one gulp.
(Roar! Gulp.)

But David was not afraid.
(Shake your head no.)

He only thought about saving the sheep.

When the lion saw that David was not afraid, it ran away, just like a big kitty cat!
(Roar? Meow!)

David went to see his brothers who were soldiers.
They were fighting with another army
whose leader was Goliath.

Goliath was so tall and strong, he looked like a giant.
(How big do you think he was?)

David said, "I fight lions all the time. I'm not afraid.
I'll fight Goliath."
(Point to yourself like David did.)

King Saul wanted David to carry a big sword,
but David said, "It's too heavy. I'll just take my sling
and some rocks."

When Goliath saw little David he laughed his giant laugh.
(Laugh loud.)

David put a stone in his sling.
(Wave your hand over your head like you have a sling.)

Snap. Crash! The stone hit Goliath and he fell down dead.
> *(Thud!)*

David saved the day!
(Hooray for David!)

When David grew up, he became the king. David was
a good king who loved the people. He won many wars.
Sometimes he did wrong things, but he asked God to
forgive him.
(Fold your hands to pray.)

God forgave him, and David tried to do better.

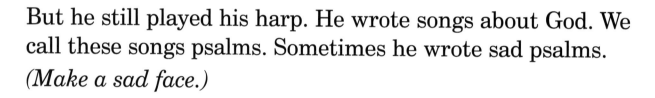

David did not watch sheep anymore.
(Shake your head no.)

But he still played his harp. He wrote songs about God. We
call these songs psalms. Sometimes he wrote sad psalms.
(Make a sad face.)

Sometimes they were all about the things God made.
(Can you name three things God made?)

One time he even wrote about a shepherd,
watching the sheep, just like he used to do.
(Baaaa.)

David was a sheep watcher and a giant killer
and song writer and a king!
(What would you like to be someday?)

David says...

You don't need to fight lions and giants to be brave. Sometimes the bravest thing to do is walk away when someone wants to start a fight. Always ask God to show you what is right.

Say a prayer with David

Dear God, thank you for all the things I can be when I grow up. Help me to be brave and good. Amen.

Fun with David

Try writing a song yourself. Hum a tune like "Mary Had a Little Lamb." Then put words to the music. Use words about people and things God has created: your family and friends, animals and mountains, flowers and trees.

Ruth Finds a Home

Naomi's husband had died and she had two sons. One son was married to Ruth. One day this son died too.

Naomi and Ruth were far from home. They had nothing to eat.
(Rub your stomach.)

They had no place to live.
(Shake your head no.)

Naomi said, "Ruth, I am going back to my family in Bethlehem. You should go back to your own land, too. Maybe we can each find food and a home."

But Ruth said, "I don't want to go without you, Naomi.
(Shake your head no.)

You are my family now. We will go together. God will give us food and a new place to live."

So Ruth and Naomi went together.
(Tap your hands on your knees for walking.)

They went to a place where the farmers left food in the field for the people who were hungry.
(Rub your stomach.)

Ruth went to the field of a man named Boaz
and picked up grain.
(Bend over to pick up grain.)

Then she made bread for Naomi.
(Pretend to fold and knead the bread.)

God had showed her how to get enough for them to eat.
(Nod yes.)

But they still did not have a home.

Boaz saw Ruth getting grain.
(Shade your eyes to look far away.)

He asked, "Who is that woman? I do not know her."
(Point to Ruth in the picture.)

His friends said, "That is Ruth. She is taking care of
Naomi. That is why she gets grain from your field."

Boaz thought Ruth was very kind to Naomi. He wanted a
wife who was kind and good. He asked Ruth to be his wife.

Ruth and Naomi moved into the big house Boaz had.
(Touch your finger tips together to make a house.)

God made sure Ruth had plenty of food
and a nice home.
(Nod your head yes.)

God had one more surprise for Ruth!
(Hold up one finger.)

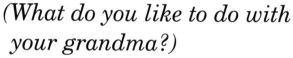

Ruth had a baby.
(Fold your arms to rock the baby.)

The women of the village named him Obed. Boaz was very
proud of his new son. Naomi loved her grandson Obed and
played with him all the time.

*(What do you like to do with
your grandma?)*

What a happy family God
gave to Ruth!

Ruth says...

Families are very important. Young or old, each person in our family should be loved and respected.

Say a prayer with Ruth

Dear God, thank you for my family. Keep everyone in my family safe, even if they are far away. Amen.

Fun with Ruth

Do you have a grandma or other family member who lives far away? Draw a picture of Naomi playing with Obed and one of that person playing with you. Put your name, address and phone number on the picture. Mail it with a note that says "I love you," and see if you get a phone call or a letter back.

Esther Saves God's People

Esther was a young Jewish girl. She loved her Uncle Mordecai. He took good care of her when she was little.

(Do you have an uncle?)

When Esther was grown up, the king of the land was looking for a new queen.

(Shade your eyes as if looking everywhere.)

Many young ladies wanted to be queen.

Each day the king met a young lady, but he never asked to see her again.

(Shake your head no.)

Then the king decided to have a contest.

Esther was smart and lovely and kind. She won the contest.

(Point to Esther in the picture.)

The king loved her at once and soon she became the queen.

Haman, the king's friend, thought he was important. He liked to have people bow to him.
(Bow like Haman wanted.)

Haman hated Uncle Mordecai because Mordecai would not bow.
(Shake your head no.)

Haman was very angry.
(Make an angry face.)

He knew Uncle Mordecai was Jewish. So he decided to get rid of Mordecai and all the Jewish people too.

Haman told the king evil lies about the Jewish people. He tricked the king into signing a law to put Mordecai and all the Jewish people to death.

Esther knew what Haman had done.

Esther wanted to see the king to tell him the truth.

But there was a problem. Anyone who went to the king without being called would be killed.

Esther was brave and trusted God. She went to see the king even though he hadn't called her.

The king was on his throne.
When he saw Esther, he smiled.
(Smile like the king.)

Esther invited the king and Haman to a big dinner
at her house.

The next day the king was very happy
with Esther's dinner.
(Rub your stomach.)

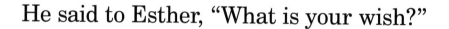

He said to Esther, "What is your wish?"

Esther whispered to the king, "Keep me and Mordecai
and all the Jewish people safe. Haman is planning
to do something very bad to us."

The king knew Esther was good and wise.

He took back the law about killing the Jewish people.
He punished Haman instead.

Everyone cheered for Queen Esther
who had saved the Jewish people!
(Hurray for Queen Esther!)

Esther says...

Sometimes it takes courage to do the right thing. But remember, God is always with you no matter how afraid you feel.

Say a prayer with Esther

Dear God, sometimes things are scary. Help me to be brave. Thank you for being with me always. Amen.

Fun with Esther

Divide a paper circle into six sections. In each section write a way to face a scary situation: talk to a grownup, run away, pray, draw a picture about it, plan a way to solve the problem, wait until it goes away. When you are afraid, bring your circle to your mom, dad or guardian. Talk together about the best thing to do.

God Saves Daniel and Jonah

Daniel was a friend of the king. He was fair and good. Many people liked him and were glad he helped the king.

(Nod your head yes.)

But there were people who did not like Daniel.

(Shake your head no.)

They made up stories about him.

Once the people who did not love God tried to trick the king. They knew Daniel would only worship the one true God.

(Hold up one finger.)

So they told the king to make a new law. The law said that everyone must worship the king as the only god. Daniel knew the king was not God. So Daniel would not worship the king.

(Shake your head no.)

Daniel was put into a deep pit with hungry, roaring lions.

(Roar!)

Daniel was not afraid. He prayed to God to save him.
(Fold your hands to pray.)

The king ran to look into the pit. Daniel was not hurt.
The lions purred like big cats.
(Purr.)

The king told all the people to worship the God
who had saved Daniel.
(Hooray! Daniel is safe.)

Another time God told Jonah to take a message
to the people. Instead Jonah ran away.
(Tap your hands on your knees. Jonah ran very fast.)

He got on a boat and sailed far away.

One night a big storm came up. The wind blew and blew.
(Blow hard and harder.)

Jonah was thrown into the sea.
(Help!)

A fish with a big mouth swam by. He swallowed water and
seaweed and little fish and Jonah.
(Gulp!)

The fish swam for three days with Jonah inside him.
*(Place palms together with fingers pointing away
from you and wiggle your hands like a fish.)*

Jonah was afraid but he prayed to God for help.
(Fold your hands to pray.)

God heard Jonah's prayer and he told the big fish
to let Jonah go.

Then the big fish swam up to a beach. Out of his big mouth
he spit water and seaweed and little fish and Jonah!

Jonah was safe on dry land.
(Whew!)

Again God asked Jonah to take a message to the people.
This time Jonah said yes!
(Nod your head yes.)

He had learned that when we love and obey God,
everything works out for the best.

Daniel and Jonah say...

God is with you even in the strangest places. God never, never leaves you alone because he loves you.

Say a prayer with Daniel and Jonah

Dear God, I know you are with me in happy times and in scary times. Thank you for loving me so much. Amen.

Fun with Daniel and Jonah

Draw a lion head and a big fish on paper plates. Tape the plates to two unsharpened pencils to make puppets. Use the puppets to tell the stories of Daniel and Jonah to a friend.

Elijah Trusts God

Elijah was a man who trusted God. Once, there was no rain for a long time. Many people were hungry. Elijah was hungry too.

(Rub your stomach.)

God told Elijah, "Go to that house. If the woman who lives there will share her food with you, I will feed you until the rain comes."

The woman said to Elijah, "I only have a little flour and oil left.

(Hold your hands close together to show "little.")

I'll make one last loaf of bread. Then my son and I will have nothing left to eat."

Elijah said, "Trust God and share your bread with me."

So the woman used up all the flour and oil in her jars to make some bread for Elijah.

Then Elijah said, "Now make some bread for you and your son."

 The woman thought the jars were empty, but when she went to look again there was enough flour and oil to make one more loaf of bread.

(Hold your hands for "little.")

After that God put flour and oil in the jars every day.

Elijah and the woman and her son had enough to eat until the rains came.

Another time, Elijah met some people who prayed to many gods.

They thought their gods were stronger than Elijah's God.

(Make a fist. How strong are you?)

Elijah had a contest. The people built a big pile of wood.

(Hold your hands to show a big pile of wood.)

Elijah built a big pile of wood.

(Hold your hands to show a big pile of wood.)

The people prayed that their gods would light the wood on fire. They prayed once.

(Hold up one finger.)

There was no smoke. They prayed twice.
(Hold up two fingers.)

There was no little flame.

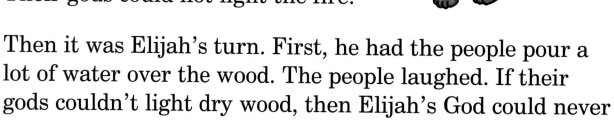

Their gods could not light the fire.

Then it was Elijah's turn. First, he had the people pour a lot of water over the wood. The people laughed. If their gods couldn't light dry wood, then Elijah's God could never get wet wood to burn.

Next Elijah prayed that God would show the people that they should trust God.

As soon as Elijah finished his prayer,
the whole pile of wet wood burst into flames!
(Wave your arms to show the big flames.)

Then all the people knew that Elijah's God
was the only true God.

Elijah says...

Sometimes a problem seems too big for anyone to fix. Trust God with the biggest problems you have. God can solve them!

Say a prayer with Elijah

Dear God, how glad I am that you always hear my prayers! I trust you with all my heart. Amen.

Fun with Elijah

Bake some bread or cookies with your family. Make up a prayer of thanks. Start out: "God, we thank you for...." Then ask the members of your family to name all the good things God gives them. How long will your prayer be?

Elizabeth and Zechariah

Elizabeth and Zechariah loved God. They were waiting for the new king God had promised to send. Many people were anxious for the new king to come. Zechariah prayed that God would send him soon.

(Fold your hands to pray.)

Elizabeth prayed for the new king too.
But she also prayed to have a baby of her own.
(Fold your arms to rock the baby.)

One day an angel came to visit Zechariah.

The angel said, "Elizabeth will have a baby. Name the baby John. When he grows up, he will help people get ready for the new king."

Zechariah said, "I am old and my wife is old.
How can we have a baby?"
(Shrug.)

The angel said, "God sent me to bring you this good news, but you did not believe me.

Now you will not be able to talk until the baby is born."
(Touch your lips. No talking.)

And from that day on Zechariah could not talk.
(Shake your head no.)

Even when Elizabeth told him the wonderful news
that she was going to have a baby,
Zechariah could say nothing at all.

Elizabeth had a cousin named Mary.

One day Mary came to visit.
She was going to have a baby too.
(Hold up two fingers for two new babies.)

When Elizabeth saw Mary she knew that the baby Mary
was going to have was the new king. How happy she was!
(Smile.)

Elizabeth and Mary talked and laughed together
and thanked God for their babies.
(Fold your hands to thank God for these babies.)

Soon Elizabeth had her baby. She loved him very much.
(Fold your arms to rock the baby.)

Everyone came to see the new baby. They said, "He will be called Zechariah, like his father."

But Elizabeth said, "No."

Everyone went to ask Zechariah about the new baby's name.

Zechariah still could not talk so he wrote, "His name is John."

Suddenly Zechariah was able to speak again! He began to praise God.

Everyone was surprised to hear him speak. *(Look surprised.)*

Everyone was glad to see the new baby. *(Smile.)*

Everyone wondered what baby John would grow up to be. They could see that God was with him in a special way.

Elizabeth and Zechariah say...

What God has promised, God will do, even if people don't think it's possible. How good it is to feel God is in charge of everything!

Say a prayer with Elizabeth and Zechariah

Dear God, you are good and loving.
Help me to trust you in everything that
happens to me. Amen.

Fun with Elizabeth and Zechariah

Everyone has a different name. Write the letters of your name down the side of a paper. Now think of a word that begins with each letter. Here's an example: JOHN might be Jump, Orange, Hen, Nickel.

Mary Is Jesus' Mother

Mary, Elizabeth's cousin, was going to marry a good man named Joseph.

One day Mary had a surprise visitor. It was an angel of God.
(Open your eyes wide.)

The angel said, "Don't be afraid, Mary. God loves you.
(Hug yourself.)

God wants you to be the mother of his son.
His son will be the new king.
You will have a baby and call him Jesus."

Mary did not understand how she could be the mother of God's son.
(Shake your head.)

But Mary said, "I will do whatever God asks."
(Fold your hands and bow like Mary did.)

One night, Joseph had a dream.
(Rest you head on your hands.)

98

An angel told him, "Joseph, God wants you to marry Mary. And here is a secret:
(Shh! Keep the secret.)

 The baby Mary will have is God's son."

Joseph obeyed the angel. He married Mary and took good care of her.

When it was almost time for Baby Jesus to be born, the emperor decided to count all the people in the land. According to the emperor's command, Mary and Joseph had to go to Bethlehem.

It was a very long trip.
(Tap your hands on your knees.)

When they got to Bethlehem, Mary and Joseph needed a place to stay. They knocked on the doors of many houses.
(Knock! Knock!)

But at each door, they heard the same thing: "No room. Go away!"

At last they found a stable to sleep in.

Joseph pushed open the door.
(Creak.)

There were some animals inside.

"Here is a warm place to stay," he told Mary.

The donkey made room for Mary to lie down and rest.
(Hee-haw.)

Very soon Jesus was born in the little stable.
It was the first Christmas!

Mary laid Jesus on the sweet hay in the cow's manger.
(Moooo.)

Soon Baby Jesus fell asleep. The funny animal noises
did not bother him.
(Rest your head on your hands.)

Mary smiled at Baby Jesus.
(Smile your happiest smile.)

Mary loved Jesus just like all mothers love their babies.
(Nod yes.)

But her baby was very special. Mary knew her baby was
God's own son! Mary knew her baby was the Savior God
had promised to send!

Mary says...

God sent his son into the world in a way that surprised everyone. On Christmas, Jesus' birthday, remember to thank God for the gift of Jesus!

Say a prayer with Mary

Dear God, thank you for your son, Jesus. I love him!
Thank you for making Mary his mother.
I love her too! Amen.

Fun with Mary

Use chenille wires or garbage bag twist ties to make figures of Baby Jesus, Mary, Joseph, and a donkey and cow. Use the figures to tell someone else the story of Christmas. Don't forget to make the animal sounds.

Jesus Has Visitors

On that first Christmas
the sheep cuddled near Jesus
to keep him warm.
(Baaaa, baaaa.)

The doves sang a pretty song
to help him sleep.
(Coooo, coooo.)

The cows were happy to let Baby Jesus
use their manger as his bed.
(Moooo, moooo.)

Soon some shepherds came running
to the barn.

They said, "We saw an angel! The angel told us,
'There is a baby in Bethlehem.
He is in a stable and he is the new king.'
(Point to Baby Jesus in the picture.)

Then, all of a sudden, the sky was full of angels.
And they were all singing and praising God!"

The shepherds were very happy to find Baby Jesus. On
their way home they told everyone they met about him.

Later, three wise men saw a special star.
(Point to the sky.)

It meant the new king had been born!
The wise men went looking for him.
Over the desert they rode on their camels.
(Galompa—galompa.)

They followed the star to Jerusalem, where King Herod
lived. Herod liked being king.
He did not want anyone else to be king.
(Shake your head no.)

The wise men went to see King Herod.
Herod told them, "When you find the new king,
come and tell me where he is. I'd like to visit him."

The wise men followed the bright star to Bethlehem.
They found Jesus with Mary and Joseph.
They gave Jesus special presents. After that God told them
in a dream not to go back to Herod.
So they went straight home.

Then Joseph had another dream.

 In the dream God's angel told him, "Hurry up, Joseph! Take Baby Jesus and Mary far away. King Herod wants to hurt Jesus. Keep him safe!"

Joseph jumped up.
(Was he hurrying?)

Joseph went over to Mary. He said, "Mary, wake up! We must leave right away.
King Herod wants to hurt Jesus."

Mary rubbed the sleep from her eyes.
(Rub your eyes.)

"Yes, Joseph," Mary said. "I will pack our clothes and get Jesus ready."

Joseph gave food and water to their little donkey.
He would need to be strong for the long trip.

Mary wrapped Baby Jesus in a warm blanket.
Then Joseph put Mary and Jesus on the donkey and they started out.

Jesus says...

Always remember that Christmas is my birthday.
Always remember that I am God's son and
I love you very much.

Say a prayer with Jesus

*Dear God, the wise men brought Jesus special
presents. I want to give Jesus a special present too—all
my love. Amen.*

Fun with Jesus

Make a tape recording of the animal sounds in this
story about Baby Jesus. Pause between sounds so you
can turn the recorder on and off. Read the story of
Baby Jesus to a friend and play the sound effects
along with it.

Joseph Keeps Jesus Safe

Mary and Jesus rode a little donkey. Joseph led the donkey by a leash. Faster and faster the little donkey went as Joseph hurried away with Mary and Jesus.

(Clippity-clop, clippity-clop.)

They did not slow down until they were in a safe place where King Herod couldn't find them. *(Whew!)*

They lived there until Jesus was a little boy. Then Joseph had another dream.

(Rest your head on your hands.)

An angel of God said, "Now it is safe to take Jesus back to your home. There he can grow up and learn everything you have to teach him."

Joseph was so happy! Mary was so happy! Jesus was so happy!

(Smile your happiest smile.)

They all went back home.

110

Now when Jesus was a little boy, he didn't eat pizza or wear blue jeans.
(Shake your head no.)

But he did grow just like all children grow,
a little every day.
And he had friends to play with.
(Who is your good friend?)

Maybe Jesus had a pet donkey.
(Hee-haw.)

Or maybe he had a puppy all his own.
(Ruff, ruff.)

When Jesus was little he learned about God from Mary and Joseph. He prayed with Mary and Joseph.

When Jesus was little he helped Mary at home.
He swept the floor.
(Swish, swish.)

When Jesus was older, he helped Joseph in the carpenter shop. He sawed wood.
(Pretend to saw.)

He pounded on nails.
(Bang, bang.)

He went to school to learn to read and write.

When Jesus grew up he told people about God his Father.
He told them all about God's love.

Many mothers and fathers wanted Jesus
to bless their children.

But some of Jesus' friends said, "Go away! Jesus is busy."
(Make an angry face.)

How sad the mothers and fathers were!
Some of the children started to cry.
(Make a sad face.)

Then Jesus said, "Stop! Bring the children to me.
I love children."

All the children ran to Jesus. They sat on his lap.
Jesus told them wonderful stories about God.

All the children were glad to be friends of Jesus.
(Smile to show you're glad to be a friend of Jesus too.)

Wherever Jesus went, children followed him. They were always happy to listen to Jesus.

Joseph says...

If you have a baby at your house, you know how wonderful it can be! Help your Mom and Dad take good care of your little brother or sister as I helped Mary take good care of Jesus.

Say a prayer with Joseph

Dear God, thank you for my family and thank you for keeping us safe wherever we go. Amen.

Fun with Joseph

Use your blocks or building toys to make three cities: the one where Jesus was born, the one where his family hid from King Herod, and the one they went to when it was safe to go home. Tell someone in your family the story about how Joseph kept Jesus safe.

John the Baptist Meets Jesus

The people who loved God were still waiting for a new king.

They didn't know yet that Jesus was the new king.

Then John, Jesus' cousin, began to talk to people by the Jordan River.

Every day many people came to listen to John.
(Touch your hand to your ear.)

John told the people to stop doing things they knew were wrong, like stealing and lying.
(Can you think of other wrong things people do?)

When the people wanted to stop doing wrong things, John took them into the River Jordan. He told them that washing with water was a sign that they wanted to change and do better.
(Pretend to wash your hands.)

The washing John did with water was called baptizing.

Now John the Baptist did not look like a king. He wore rough clothes and ate strange food like grasshoppers and wild honey. Even though he did this, many people came to listen to him.

(Point to your ears.)

John was so sure of what God wanted.

The people knew that what he said was right.

 Some of them said, "Maybe John is the new king."
(Point to John in the picture.)

John said, "I am not the new king, but I will show you who he is."

So the people kept coming every day to hear John. And they waited for the new king.

One day, Jesus came to the River Jordan from Nazareth. Jesus came to be baptized by John.

John got into the water with Jesus.

Jesus went under the water and came up again.

As Jesus came up out of the water,
John saw a bright light from heaven.
(Point up.)

Then the Holy Spirit came down like a dove over
Jesus' head.

John heard a voice. It was God saying, "This is my son,
whom I love. I am very pleased with him."

Then John knew. His cousin Jesus was the new king!

"Look!" John called out to all the people. "This is the new
king! This is the Lamb of God!"

John was happy. His job was to show the people who the
new king would be. And he did his job very well!

John says...

God always forgives us when we are sorry for the wrong things we do. It's wonderful to know that God loves us no matter what! God showed he loves us by sending Jesus into the world.

Say a prayer with John

Dear God, thank you for my baptism. In baptism you made me your child and filled me with your very own life. Help me to always live like your son Jesus. Amen.

Fun with John

John ate strange food. Name some things we don't eat today. (Here's a hint: bugs and grass.) Draw a picture of the dinner you will never eat.

Andrew Follows Jesus

Andrew was sitting beside the Jordan River.

He was listening to John the Baptist talk about the new king. *(Point to your ears.)*

John called the new king the Lamb of God. Then he pointed to Jesus, the teacher from Nazareth.

Andrew looked at Jesus. Jesus did not wear fine robes like the priests in the Temple. He did not use big words or have any servants. What kind of a king could Jesus be? *(Shrug your shoulders.)*

Andrew went up to Jesus and said, "Rabbi." That is what Andrew called anyone who was a great teacher and very wise.

Andrew listened to Jesus all day. By that night Andrew was sure Jesus was the new king, sent by God.

Andrew wanted to become a follower of Jesus. But first he had something important to do. He had to tell his brother, Simon, about Jesus. He ran to find him. *(Tap your hands on your knees for running.)*

Andrew said, "Simon, come and see! I have met the man who is the new king! It's the Rabbi Jesus."

Then Andrew and Simon became followers of Jesus.

One time Andrew helped Jesus in a special way.

Lots of people had come to hear Jesus tell about God's love. At dinner time, they were hungry.
(Rub your stomach.)

Jesus said, "Give the people something to eat."

Jesus' friends looked everywhere for some food.
(Look around. Do you see any food?)

Then Andrew brought a young boy to Jesus. "Here," Andrew said, "this boy has two fish. *(Hold up two fingers.)*

He also has five loaves of bread." *(Hold up five fingers.)*

Jesus took the bread and fish. He blessed it and fed all the people with the food Andrew had found! There were more than 5,000 people there!

(Spread your arms wide. What a lot of people!)

Andrew liked being a special follower of Jesus.

All the followers listened to Jesus talk about God's love.

Sometimes Jesus healed people. Sometimes he blessed the children.

(How old are you? Jesus blessed children your age!)

Jesus was always kind. Jesus always listened.

Andrew learned to be kind. He became a good listener too.

(Can you name someone who listens to you? Jesus always will!)

Andrew says...

Knowing Jesus is so wonderful that you'll want to tell other people about him. Maybe you can tell your brother or sister. Then you can both be Jesus' helpers.

Say a prayer with Andrew

Dear God, thank you for showing me how to be Jesus' helper. I will try to be kind and listen to others every day. Amen.

Fun with Andrew

Have a snack with five crackers and some peanut butter. Even if you can't feed more than 5,000 people, you can share what you have with a brother or sister or friend.

James and John Help Jesus

James and John were brothers. Every day they got up very early.
(Yawn. How early do you get up?)

They got into a big boat and went fishing. They worked very hard. All day long they caught fish for the people to eat.

Some were big fish.
(Hold your hands far apart.)

Some were little fish.
(Hold your hands close together.)

James and John liked to fish to help feed others.

One day when they were fishing they saw a man on the beach.
(Shade your eyes to see far away.)

They saw him wave to them and call them by name.

"James, you know how to fish for fish," the man called, "follow me and fish for people."

Who was the man on the beach?

James did not know him at all, but he wanted to hear more about fishing for people.

He put down the net he was using to fish.

He got out of the boat and went to the man on the beach. *(Splish-splash.)*

The man was Jesus.

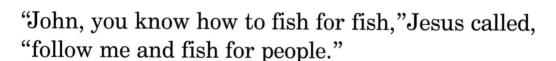

John was still in the boat.

He heard Jesus call him by name. *(Touch your ear to listen.)*

"John, you know how to fish for fish,"Jesus called, "follow me and fish for people."

John did not know Jesus, but he wanted to hear more about fishing for people.

He put down the net he was using to fish.

He got out of the boat and went to Jesus. *(Splish-splash.)*

All day long James and John listened to Jesus. They liked to hear Jesus tell about God's love for everyone. They liked to hear about the kingdom where Jesus would rule and there would be no hunger and sadness.

At the end of the day, James and John knew what to do.
(Nod yes.)

The next day they got up very early.
(Yawn.)

They went fishing, but not for fish. Now they were Jesus' helpers and they fished for people. They didn't really catch them in nets, but they helped people listen to Jesus and they told others about God's love.

Some were big people.
(Hold hands high overhead.)

Some were little people.
(Hold hands at waist level.)

James and John liked to help Jesus tell people about God's love.

James and John say...

Jesus needs helpers of all kinds. You don't need to be a grownup or even know how to fish! Just being kind and loving makes you a good helper.

Say a prayer with James and John

Dear God, I want to be like James and John and help Jesus your son. By being kind and loving I can teach others about you. Amen.

Fun with James and John

James and John liked to go fishing together. Draw a picture of something special you would like to do with a brother or sister.

Jesus Visits Mary and Martha

Mary and Martha were sisters.
They were good friends of Jesus.
Jesus liked to visit their little house.
They ate and laughed together.

One day Martha was very busy.

Sweep, sweep went Martha's broom.
(Pretend to sweep.)

Stir, stir, as she stirred the batter
for bread.
(Pretend to stir.)

Dust, dust, as she cleaned everything.
(Pretend to clean the furniture.)

Martha was getting ready for Jesus.

Mary was getting ready for Jesus too.
She picked some flowers.
(What color do you think the flowers were?)

She remembered the stories Jesus had told last time
he was with them. Mary watched for Jesus to come down
the road.
(Shade your eyes to see far away.)

134

Mary was getting ready for Jesus.

Finally Jesus arrived. When people heard that Jesus was at the little house they came to see him.
(Tap your hands on your knees.)

Soon the house was full of people.

Jesus began to teach about the love of God and how to be kind to one another.

Martha looked at all the people.
(Circle your eyes with your fingers.)

She was not happy to have the little house so full of people who wanted to see Jesus.
(Shake your head no.)

She had to make more bread and get more food. She was so busy taking care of all the people who had come that she did not have time to listen to Jesus.

Mary looked at all the people.
(Circle your eyes with your fingers.)

Mary was glad people could come to the little house to
see Jesus.
(Nod your head yes.)

She helped everyone find a seat, and then she sat down and
listened.
(Point to your ears.)

Martha was tired of all the cleaning and cooking.

She felt angry at Mary for not helping.
(Make an angry face.)

Martha said to Jesus, "Make Mary come and help me!"

Jesus said, "Martha, there will be time later to cook and
clean. God's love is for busy people like you too. After
I am gone Mary will remember the wonderful things I have
to say. Now come and sit by me. I have so much
to tell you."
(Point to a chair beside you.)

Mary and Martha say...

Every day you have lots of things to do. But always remember the most important things. Remember to take time to learn more about Jesus and God's love. Remember to say your prayers.

Say a prayer with Mary and Martha

Dear God, thank you for the Bible where I can hear about the life of Jesus and learn more about your love. Keep me busy loving you and helping others. Amen.

Fun with Mary and Martha

What if Jesus visited your house? What important things would you show him? What would you tell him or ask him? Remember, Jesus is always with you because he lives in your heart. You can talk to him anytime by praying.

Bartimaeus Can See!

Bartimaeus was a beggar who liked to sit by the side of the road. He listened to the people walking by. *(Tap your hands on your knees.)*

He could feel the warm sun on his back.

He could smell the fresh bread baking. *(Sniff. What do you smell?)*

He liked to pet the noses of donkeys as they passed.

Bartimaeus wished only for one thing.
He wished he could see.

Bartimaeus was not able to use his eyes so he could never see all the wonderful things around him.
(Close your eyes. That's how dark it was for Bartimaeus all the time!)

One day the crowd on the road was very noisy. People told Bartimaeus, "Jesus, the teacher, is coming this way."

Jesus! Bartimaeus had heard about Jesus.

People said Jesus could make sick persons well. They said he had made a person who was deaf able to hear again.
(Point to your ears.)

Bartimaeus wondered, "Could Jesus help me see?"
(Point to your eyes.)

Bartimaeus heard the crowd come closer and closer.

Bartimaeus had to shout to be heard over the noise.

"Jesus," he called out, "have mercy on me!"

Jesus kept on walking.
(Tap hands on knees.)

The people closest to Bartimaeus whispered, "Be quiet!"
(Shhh!)

Bartimaeus was sure that if he could just talk to Jesus, Jesus would help him see.

So he shouted in his loudest voice.
"Jesus, have mercy on me!"

Jesus stopped walking.
(Tap hands on knees, then stop.)

The people near Bartimaeus said,
"Hurry, Bartimaeus! Jesus wants you!"

They helped Bartimaeus find Jesus.

Jesus said, "What do you want me to do for you?"

Bartimaeus said, "I want to see."

Jesus touched Bartimaeus' eyes.
(Touch your eyes.)

All of a sudden Bartimaeus could see the people!
(Are there people where you are?)

He could see the sunshine! He could see a loaf of bread!
He could see the soft nose of a donkey!

But the first thing he saw was the very best thing.
It was Jesus' smiling face!
(Smile your biggest smile.)

Bartimaeus was so happy to be able to see
that he told everyone he met about how
Jesus had helped him.

Bartimaeus says...

Jesus helped me see with my eyes. Many people who can't see can wear glasses. God always gives us the help that we need to live and serve others.

Say a prayer with Bartimaeus

Dear God, thank you for my eyes and ears and nose and tongue and fingers. Thank you for every part of me! Amen.

Fun with Bartimaeus

Try walking slowly through your house with your eyes closed. (Make sure someone is with you to keep you from bumping into something or hurting yourself.) Or try to ask for a drink of water without using your tongue. Is there someone you know who is physically challenged? How can you be a good neighbor to that person?

Zacchaeus Finds a Friend

Zacchaeus had been busy collecting taxes. He took some money for the Romans, but he took extra money for himself.

Zacchaeus was very rich. His money made him happy.
(Smile like Zacchaeus did.)

People knew Zacchaeus took extra money for himself. They did not like that. So Zacchaeus did not have any friends.
(Shake your head no.)

Zacchaeus thought he would like to have a friend, but he liked the money more. So he kept taking extra money for himself.
(Rub your hands together.)

One day Zacchaeus heard that a new teacher was coming to town. It was someone named Jesus.

Zacchaeus had heard about Jesus healing others.

But Zacchaeus didn't think he needed to be healed.
(*Shake your head no.*)

Zacchaeus heard that Jesus talked about sharing.

But Zacchaeus did not want to share.
(*Shake your head no.*)

Then someone said, "Jesus is so kind.
He is a friend to everyone."

Zacchaeus wondered, "Could Jesus become my friend?"

So he went to see Jesus. But so did everyone else in town.
All the people stood along the road and waved to Jesus.
(*Wave your arms high.*)

Zacchaeus couldn't see anything because he was short.

Then Zacchaeus had a great idea. He climbed up 1-2-3
branches into a tree. Now he could see over all
the other people.
(*Shade your eyes to see far away.*)

But would Jesus see Zacchaeus?

Zacchaeus was very surprised when Jesus stopped under the tree and looked up.

(Look up.)

Jesus said, "Zacchaeus, come down. I am going to eat dinner at your house today."

Zacchaeus could hardly believe his ears!

He climbed down one branch.
(Hold up one finger.)

He knew he wanted Jesus to be his friend.

He climbed down two branches.
(Hold up two fingers.)

He knew he did not want to cheat people anymore by taking extra money for himself.

He climbed down three branches.
(Hold up three fingers.)

Zacchaeus knew what he had to do. He would give back all the money he had taken that did not belong to him. He would never take more for himself again. And he would have lots of friends!

Jesus liked Zacchaeus' plan.

They went home to dinner together as two good friends.

Zacchaeus says...

It's best to play fair and never cheat anyone, even if it's just in a game. Kind and honest people make God happy and have more friends.

Say a prayer with Zacchaeus

Dear God, thank you for sending Jesus into the world to be the best friend we could have. Amen.

Fun with Zacchaeus

On a long piece of paper, draw a tall tree. Draw a person in the branches. That's Zacchaeus. Draw a man on the ground. That is Jesus. Can you use the picture to tell someone else the story about the two friends?

Peter Learns to Be a Follower of Jesus

After Andrew's brother Simon became a follower of Jesus, Jesus changed his name to Peter.

Of all Jesus' followers, Peter was the loudest. Peter asked the most questions. He was first in line whenever Jesus needed helpers.
(Hold up one finger.)

Peter liked to hear Jesus talk about heaven and the kingdom where Jesus would be king. Lots of people liked to hear this.
(Nod yes.)

But some powerful people were not happy with Jesus.
(Shake your head no.)

They thought that if Jesus was king they would lose their power. So they made plans to take Jesus away from his friends.

One night, Jesus had a special supper with his friends.

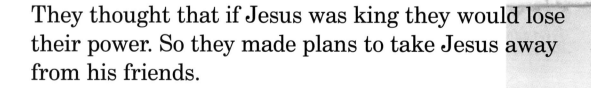

152

Peter sat close to Jesus. Jesus blessed bread and wine and gave it to his friends. The bread and wine were now Jesus' own Body and Blood!

Then Jesus said, "I will have to leave you."

Peter said loudly, "I'm your friend forever!"
(Point to yourself like Peter did.)

Jesus sadly told Peter, "Soon you will say you don't even know me."

Peter said, "I would never say that!"
(Shake your head no.)

Not long after, some powerful people did take Jesus away. Jesus' friends were afraid. They ran and hid. Peter waited outside the place where Jesus was.

Some people asked him if he knew Jesus.
Three times Peter said, "I don't know him at all!"
(Hold up three fingers.)

Then some men nailed Jesus to a cross. Jesus died on the cross to save us from our sins. But Jesus is God. In three days, he came back to life again!

After Jesus came back to life, he saw Peter fishing.

Peter ran through the water to meet Jesus on the beach.
(Wiggle your fingers for the waves.)

Peter wondered, "Will Jesus be angry at me for saying
I didn't know him?"

But Jesus was not angry at all.

He was very kind and forgiving.

Jesus asked Peter three times, "Can you take care of the
people who love me as if you are a shepherd and they are
sheep?"
(Hold up three fingers.)

Three times Peter said, "Yes, Lord."
(Nod yes.)

Peter loved Jesus so much that he promised to spend all his
time telling everyone about Jesus and God's love.

Peter didn't say it loudly that time,
but he meant it with all his heart!
(Put your hands over your heart.)

Peter says...

What's important is not how loud you say things, but how much you mean them. Jesus will help you mean what you say and love others.

Say a prayer with Peter

Dear God, telling the truth is not always easy, but I know that I can always do it with your help. Amen.

Fun with Peter

Peter liked to be loud. For fun, talk through an old paper towel tube. Can you be very loud? Very soft? What voice is best for telling others, "Jesus loves you"?

Paul Believes in Jesus

After Jesus went to be with God in heaven, many of his helpers told others about him.

Some people liked what Jesus' friends had to say.
(Smile.)

But some people did not like this news.
(Make an angry face.)

Jesus was not the kind of king they wanted so they did not want him to be the king at all. They wanted to stop those who believed in Jesus from telling other people about him.

Sometimes they put Jesus' followers in jail. Sometimes they threw rocks at them. One day a man named Saul was going to a city where people lived who loved Jesus. Saul was going to stop them from teaching about Jesus. He was riding his horse very fast.
(Tap your hands on your knees very fast.)

Suddenly there was a bright light and a loud noise.
(Clap as loud as you can.)

Saul fell down. He heard a voice say, "Saul, Saul, why do you hurt the people who love me?"

"Who are you?" Saul asked.

The voice answered, "I am Jesus, and whenever you hurt one of my friends, you hurt me. Go into the city and you will find out what to do next."

Then the light went away.

Saul was sitting on the ground. His eyes were open but he couldn't see. Saul was blind!
(Cover your eyes and keep them covered.)

A friend had to take him by the hand and bring him to the city. In the city Saul stayed at a kind man's house.

A few days later, a man who loved Jesus came to visit Saul.

The man put his hands on Saul's eyes. All of a sudden Saul could see again!
(Uncover your eyes. How nice to be able to see again!)

Saul told everyone that he had seen Jesus. Now he believed that Jesus truly was the king, the son of God.

Saul said he was changing his name to Paul. From then on he spent his time telling others about God's love and about Jesus, God's son.

Some people liked what Paul had to say.
(Smile.)

But some people did not like this news.
(Make an angry face.)

They tried to put Paul in jail or even kill him. But Paul would not stop talking about Jesus and God's love.

Paul says...

Jesus wants us all to be his helpers and tell others about God's love. Who can you tell this good news to?

Say a prayer with Paul

Dear God, make me brave to tell others about your love. It is the good news we all need to hear. Amen.

Fun with Paul

Paul traveled all over the world telling others about Jesus. At the time Paul lived some of the most important places were what are now Israel and Palestine, Greece, Syria and Italy. Can you find those places on a map? Where would you like to go to tell others about God's love?

Lydia Helps Paul

Lydia lived by the sea.

At that time most women were wives and mothers, but Lydia was also a trader. She made and sold purple cloth to people who came to her town.

(Are you wearing any purple?)

The people who bought Lydia's purple cloth showed it to others. Soon lots of people wanted Lydia's beautiful cloth. She was very busy and very rich.

One day Lydia and her friends sat beside the sea.

They had a special place they liked to go to pray and talk.
(Wiggle your fingers along the ground like the waves on the sea.)

They looked far into the distance.
(Shade your eyes to look far away.)

There was a man coming to talk to them.
Maybe he wanted to buy some purple cloth.

The man said, "My name is Paul. I've come to tell you about God's love. God loves everyone!"
(Point to people in the room with you. God loves them all!)

Lydia and her friends were surprised by that news.
(Can you look surprised?)

Lydia thought the God of Israel only loved some people. She didn't know that he loved the people in her town too. Now Paul was saying that the God of Israel is the God who loves everyone. How was that possible?
(Shrug your shoulders.)

Paul told Lydia and her friends that because Jesus had died and come back to life for all people, God's love was for everyone.
(Hug yourself. Jesus loves you, too.)

Lydia and her friends were very happy to hear this good news!

Lydia said, "Please come stay at my house, Paul, and tell others this wonderful news."
(Touch your fingertips together to make a house.)

Every day Paul taught the people who came to Lydia's house.

Sometimes just a few close friends were there.

At other times so many people came to hear the good news that they had to sit outside.
(Point out the window.)

Lydia kept selling her purple cloth, but she gave the money to Paul.

After everyone in Lydia's town had heard Paul, he used the money to travel far away to tell others about God's love. Everyone needed to hear that good news!

Everyone today need to hear it too!
(Spread your arms wide to tell everybody about God's love.)

Lydia says...

I was so glad to hear about God's love for me and for my family. Paul was a good friend to tell me.
Do you have a good friend you could tell about God's love?

Say a prayer with Lydia

Dear God, thank you for loving me just as I am. Amen

Fun with Lydia

On a paper write "God loves you and so do I." Don't sign it. Leave the note under someone's plate at dinner. What wonderful news they will get. Will they guess the note is from you?

Timothy Works with Paul

Paul traveled to many places telling people about Jesus and God's love.

Sometimes he walked.

Sometimes he sailed on a ship with big sails. The wind blew Paul to many different countries.

(Blow hard like the wind.)

Paul wanted to travel all over the world to tell people about Jesus. He wanted to teach all people that God loves them. But he was only one person.

(Hold up one finger.)

Paul needed helpers.

One friend who helped Paul was Timothy. Timothy learned about Jesus when he was a little boy.

(How old are you? Maybe Timothy was your age when he first heard about Jesus.)

Timothy's mother was named Eunice.
His grandmother was named Lois.

(Do you know your mother's name?)

Eunice and Lois taught Timothy all about Jesus. They told him that Jesus is kind and wants everyone to share.

Timothy tried to be kind like Jesus.
He shared his things with other children.
(What things can you share?)

Eunice and Lois told Timothy that Jesus always forgives.
(When someone hurts you, do you try to forgive like Jesus?)

Timothy learned to live like Jesus.

When Paul met Timothy's family, he knew Timothy would be a good helper. Paul asked Timothy to help him teach about Jesus.

Timothy traveled with Paul to many new places.
Sometimes they walked. Sometimes they sailed on big ships.

(How would you like to travel?)

There were so many people who wanted to hear about Jesus! How could Paul and Timothy talk to more of them?

They decided to go alone to different cities and teach.

Paul and Timothy liked to be together. They knew they would miss each other. But Paul had a plan.

They did not have telephones.
(Hold your hand up to your ear as if talking on the phone.)

They did not have computers.
(Pretend to type.)

So they decided to write letters to each other.

Paul wrote letters to remind Timothy to be like Jesus and serve others and help the poor.

Even when Paul was put in jail by some people who didn't want him to teach about Jesus, he wrote to his friend Timothy.

Timothy liked to get letters from Paul.
(Who do you like to get letters from?)

Timothy says...

Paul's letters really helped me. The words Paul wrote to me are in the Bible in the books of the New Testament with my name, 1 Timothy and 2 Timothy. Maybe you would like to read them.

Say a prayer with Timothy

Dear God, thank you for leaders like Paul. Help them guide us to be kind and loving, just like Jesus. Amen.

Fun with Timothy

It's always fun to get mail! Write a letter to someone you don't see very often. Tell them what you are doing and remind them that you love them, and that Jesus does too!

About the Author

Robin Currie holds a Master of Divinity degree as well as a Masters in Library Science. An experienced children's librarian and bookseller, she is currently serving as a parish director of children's and family ministries. Robin has authored resources for teachers and librarians in addition to Bible stories and children's religious education curricula. She lives with her family in the suburbs of Chicago.

 *Pauline* BOOKS & MEDIA

CALIFORNIA
3908 Sepulveda Blvd., Culver City, CA 90230; 310-397-8676
5945 Balboa Ave., San Diego, CA 92111; 619-565-9181
46 Geary Street, San Francisco, CA 94108; 415-781-5180

FLORIDA
145 S.W. 107th Ave., Miami, FL 33174; 305-559-6715

HAWAII
1143 Bishop Street, Honolulu, HI 96813; 808-521-2731

ILLINOIS
172 North Michigan Ave., Chicago, IL 60601; 312-346-4228

LOUISIANA
4403 Veterans Memorial Blvd., Metairie, LA 70006;
504-887-7631

MASSACHUSETTS
50 St. Paul's Ave., Jamaica Plain, Boston, MA 02130;
617-522-8911
Rte. 1, 885 Providence Hwy., Dedham, MA 02026;
781-326-5385

MISSOURI
9804 Watson Rd., St. Louis, MO 63126; 314-965-3512

NEW JERSEY
561 U.S. Route 1, Wick Plaza, Edison, NJ 08817;
732-572-1200

NEW YORK
150 East 52nd Street, New York, NY 10022; 212-754-1110
78 Fort Place, Staten Island, NY 10301; 718-447-5071

OHIO
2105 Ontario Street, Cleveland, OH 44115; 216-621-9427

PENNSYLVANIA
9171-A Roosevelt Blvd., Philadelphia, PA 19114;
215-676-9494

SOUTH CAROLINA
243 King Street, Charleston, SC 29401; 803-577-0175

TENNESSEE
4811 Poplar Ave., Memphis, TN 38117; 901-761-2987

TEXAS
114 Main Plaza, San Antonio, TX 78205; 210-224-8101

VIRGINIA
1025 King Street, Alexandria, VA 22314; 703-549-3806

CANADA
3022 Dufferin Street, Toronto, Ontario, Canada M6B 3T5;
416-781-9131
1155 Yonge Street, Toronto, Ontario, Canada M4T 1W2;
416-934-3440